Cristia

The Inspirational Story of Soccer (Football) Superstar Cristiano Ronaldo

Table Of Contents

Introduction

As the title already implies, this is a short book about [The Inspirational Story of Football Superstar Cristiano Ronaldo] and how he rose from his life in Portugal to become one of today's leading and most-respected football players. In his rise to superstardom, Cristiano has inspired not only the youth, but fans of all ages throughout the world.

This book also portrays the struggles that Cristiano has had to overcome during his early childhood years, his teen years, and up until he became what he is today. A notable source of inspiration is Cristiano's service to the community and his strong connection with the fans of the sport. He continues to serve as a polarizing, entertaining superstar in a sport that certainly needs it.

Combining incredible mental fortitude, impeccable mechanics, an aggressive play style, and high football IQ, Cristiano has shown the ability to completely dominate a match. From being a young boy who dedicated his free time to the football field to becoming one of the greatest football players of all-time, you'll learn here how this man has risen the ranks.

Thanks again for grabbing this book. Hopefully you can take some of the examples and lessons from Cristiano's story and apply them to your own   life!

Chapter 1:

Youth & Family Life

Cristiano Ronaldo dos Santos Aveiro was welcomed into the world on February 5th, 1985 in Funchal, Madeira, Portugal. Born to father, Jose Aviero, and mother, Maria Dolores Aveiro, Cristiano is the youngest child of the family. Cristiano's second name, "Ronaldo", was given to him at birth after his father's favorite actor, and then-president of the United States, Ronald Reagan.

Cristiano has two elder sisters, Elma and Liliana Catia, as well as one older brother, Hugo. As an interesting aside, Cristiano's great-grandmother, Isabel da Piedade, was a native of Cape Verde. Growing up, the family got by on modest means and learned to find joy in the simple things. In fact, Cristiano himself would tell later on that he and his family lived in poverty. Cristiano was raised in a Catholic household and he learned to be humble at a young age. Of course, this attitude and worldview would stick with him even as he advanced in age and achieved superstardom.

While Jose had positive intentions and tried to be a strong family man, he often struggled to control his drinking habit. In fact, it is this same problem that unfortunately caused his early demise in 2005, due to kidney issues secondary to alcohol abuse. Maria served as a strong woman and was always an incredible role model for Cristiano and his siblings. She worked long hours at her cooking and cleaning jobs, while also making sure the children were fed and well taken care of.

In spite of his personal struggles, Jose did have a strong relationship with Cristiano and served an integral role in his son's future in athletics. Jose worked as the equipment manager at a boy's club while his children were growing up.

Through Jose's job, Cristiano was introduced to the sport of football at a very young age. Cristiano played for Andorinha, a local amateur team, when he was eight years old.

By the time he hit ten years of age, Cristiano was already highly competitive and clearly gifted in the sport. His godfather, Fernao Sousa, said that all young Cristiano wanted as a boy was to play football. This combination of drive and talent would push him to become proficient at the sport quickly. It wouldn't be long until Cristiano was considered a "child phenom" among his peers.

In school, Cristiano was a popular classmate but possessed a polarizing personality. After a teacher disrespected him in class, Cristiano threw a chair at him - resulting in expulsion. By the time Cristiano was fourteen years of age, he convinced his mother that he would put his entire focus on excelling at football. He told her that he is maybe good enough to play at least semi-professionally, and that he should take a chance, by focusing entirely on the game. One advantage Cristiano possessed over other children was that he had always been a highly self-motivated individual. So much so, that he would even skip his mother's meals or sneak out of his room when it was homework time, just to continue improving his game.

He soon became completely infatuated with all aspects of the game - whether it was learning the fundamentals, developing his mental toughness, or watching others play. This obsession with being around the field stuck with Cristiano throughout his life, as he developed a passion for the intricacies of the sport.

By the time he reached his early teenage years, he was becoming a sure-fire talent that club teams and fans around the world were drooling over. In 2001, after a short run with local club, Nacional da liha da Madeira, including a title victory, Cristiano signed with Sporting Portugal, one of the most prominent professional teams in Portugal. Signed for an undisclosed amount,

Sporting made the move to acquire his services after an impressive showing during a 3-day trial with the club.

Signing with Sporting meant that Cristiano had to leave behind his family in Madeira and learn how to cope with life on his own. This early exposure to independence only made him tougher. During his early days with the squad, Cristiano trained with his peers at the Academia Sporting football academy in Alcochete.

Cristiano's peers in this academy included names who later on became professionals themselves. Of course, just like most of the best do, he found a way to stand out among his peers. He would later go on to become the only player in the history of the organization to play for the U-16, U-17, U-18, B-Team and First Team, all in a single season (2002).

An unexpected setback came Cristiano's way when he was fifteen. He was diagnosed with a racing heart - a life-threatening condition that could have possibly forced him to give up playing the sport he loved dearly. After Sporting Portugal's staff notified Cristiano's mother of the diagnosis, Cristiano was admitted to a hospital for a surgical procedure. Cristiano's heart was operated on by a laser in the early morning, cauterizing the area that was causing his condition.

By the end of the afternoon, Cristiano was discharged from the hospital. Remarkably, he was cleared and went back to training only a few days later. This close call motivated Cristiano even further, showing him how lucky he was to be able to play the sport that he loved, and more importantly, how quickly it could be taken away from him.

Needless to say, these powerful events in his early life shaped Cristiano Ronaldo both as a player and as a person. Even at an early age, his immense talents, his relentless work ethic, his incredible drive, and his big heart has been on display. As he became a professional, he would carry these traits with him, to become one of the biggest personalities in football, both on and off the pitch.

Chapter 2:

Professional Life

Cristiano Ronaldo's professional career officially started in 2002. At the age of 16, he made his debut with Sporting CP's First Team. He immediately made an impression in his first appearance, scoring 2 goals in Sporting's 3-0 win against Moreirense.

Proving that this stellar debut was not a fluke, he consistently put up impressive performances throughout the season. Some of his most dazzling outings came against some of the best teams. During that same year, he also played for Portugal in the Under-17 European Championship. His footwork and ball-handling skills stood out, making an impression on fans and players alike. His stint with Sporting CP was so impressive that soon, the biggest professional clubs all over the world came knocking at Sporting's door for his services.

In November 2002, Cristiano and his representatives were invited to Arsenal FC's training grounds to meet with long-time Arsenal coach, Arsene Wenger. Though no signing took place, Liverpool FC was also in the mix in signing him.

Manchester United also joined the bidding wars soon after Cristiano led Sporting to a 3-1 win over Manchester United in Lisbon. In fact, it was some of the United players who tried to convince their legendary manager Sir Alex Ferguson to sign the young stud they had just competed against, saying that he is one of the most exciting young players they'd ever seen. Not long afterwards, the club decided to fork out over twelve million pounds to acquire Cristiano's services - a record pay-out for a talent of his age.

With this record signing, Cristiano became the first Portuguese player to ever play for Manchester United. United manager, Alex Ferguson, assigned him the jersey number 7 - previously worn by United legends such as George Best, Bryan Robson, Eric Cantona, and David Beckham.

Originally, Cristiano requested to wear number twenty-eight, his jersey number at Sporting, but Ferguson insisted that Cristiano should wear number seven as an extra source of motivation. With this assignment, Cristiano was basically forced to live up to the challenge. This, combined with the huge cost of signing him, automatically made Cristiano one of the most-hyped newcomers in Manchester United history.

His debut for Manchester United came in November 2003, during a 4-0 home victory over the Bolton Wanderers. Cristiano entered the game in the sixtieth minute, with the United fans at Old Trafford giving him a standing ovation. He showed what he could do right away, surprisingly unnerved in his new position and the pressure that came along with it.

Ferguson called the performance "marvelous", while George Best said that Cristiano was "special". Among other things, Cristiano brought a new dimension to the team - the ability to spring quickly from defense into an offensive attack. This is no small feat, as Manchester United still featured a loaded squad back then, including the likes of Roy Keane, Ryan Giggs, Paul Scholes, and Ruud van Nistelrooy.

Cristiano's first scored goal came on a free kick as part of a 3-0 victory against Portsmouth on November 1st. Despite showing improvement throughout the season, Cristiano did not score another goal until March 20th against Tottenham Hotspur. For the rest of his first campaign with United, Cristiano scored two more goals - an equalizer in a 2-1 victory against Birmingham City, and the opener in a 2-0 victory against Aston Villa, on the final day of the season. The game against Aston Villa also marked the first red card of Cristiano's career.

That season, Manchester United did not win the English Premier League (Arsenal did in record-setting fashion, finishing the season without a loss in 38 games). However, with a deep squad and led by a future great in Cristiano Ronaldo, fans of the Red Devils knew they have something to look forward to.

While his Premier League season was more or less an up-and-down one, the 2003-04 FA Cup somewhat turned into Cristiano Ronaldo's coming-out party for Manchester United. In the fifth round of the 2003-04 FA Cup, Cristiano scored a goal as part of a 4-2 victory over Manchester City. Cristiano finished the season on a high note, scoring the opening goal in United's 3-0 victory over Millwall in the FA Cup Final. This timely performance by the young star earned him high praise from all around the world.

In the summer of 2004, Cristiano played for the senior team of Portugal. Called up to play in Euro 2004 (where Portugal was the host), he scored his first goal of the tournament in a 2-1 group stage loss to Greece and another in a 2-1 semifinal victory over the Netherlands. Portugal went all the way to the finals, losing to Greece once again, 1-0.

After finishing with two goals and two assists for the tournament, Cristiano was announced as part of the UEFA Euro All-Star team. In the summer of 2004, Cristiano represented Portugal at the 2004 Olympics. The team did not perform well, finishing at the bottom of its group and eventually eliminated in the first round of competition. Cristiano scored one goal in tournament play.

Needless to say, with a successful first season, expectations were quite high at Old Trafford. Cristiano did not score a goal in his second season with United until December, when he added the third goal in a 3-0 victory over Southampton. Nonetheless, Cristiano was showing an obvious improvement in his second campaign, especially in his comfortability in attacking. He had really begun to settle into the team's approach and was putting constant pressure on the defense by the beginning of 2005.

Two other notable performances during the 2004-05 season came when Cristiano scored two goals in a 4-2 victory over defending champions Arsenal and the only goal in a victory over Fulham - from twenty-five yards away. After the game against Fulham, Ferguson called Cristiano the team's best player. Cristiano showed his clutch abilities once again, scoring four goals during the team's 2005 FA Cup run. However, they lost the FA Cup final to Arsenal on penalties.

At this point, Cristiano was considered one of the faces of Manchester United. He was also becoming a fan-favorite – not just because of his impressive performances, but also because of his intense personality, relentless playing style, and good looks. As the 2005-06 season approached, Cristiano reached a point where there were noticeably high expectations from media outlets around Europe.

The 2005-06 season saw Cristiano score United's 1,000th Premier League goal as part of a 4-1 loss to Middlesbrough. Additionally, Cristiano scored three braces during the campaign, against Bolton, Fulham, and Portsmouth. In November, United made sure to commit to Cristiano by signing him to a contract extension for two more years, which would keep him playing for the team until 2010. Naturally, Cristiano was happy with the development, saying that staying with the club was "important for the development of his career".

In spite of this early success, there were a lot of rough patches for Cristiano Ronaldo, both on and off the field. UEFA suspended him for one match because he showed the fans the middle finger during a UEFA Champions League match against Benfica. Also, he received a red card in a match against Manchester City (a match they went on to lose 3-1) for kicking Andy Cole.

However, his most dramatic dust-up that year was his feud with Ruud van Nistelrooy. Clashing for the entire season, Ronaldo and Van Nistelrooy even had a fight during practice. At the end of the season, Van Nistelrooy signed with Real Madrid.

Those last two seasons were rough for Cristiano. Aside from the aforementioned controversies, his game was still very much raw, still prone to errors and poor decision making. Aside from this, he had only won one championship: the 2006 Football League Cup. Still, Cristiano slowly rose up to relevancy amongst casual football fans. His rise was boosted tremendously by a great showing during the Eastern zone qualifier for the 2006 FIFA World Cup. Cristiano scored seven goals and was the second-highest scorer of that zonal qualifiers.

Cristiano scored his first goal in World Cup competition against Iran, as part of a 2-0 Portugal victory. However, controversy ensued in Portugal's quarterfinal match against England. Cristiano and United teammate and friend, Wayne Rooney, were involved in a controversial decision regarding Rooney's ejection, after stomping on Portuguese player Ricardo Carvalho.

After the match, there was speculation from the English media that Rooney was sent off because of Cristiano's complaints. However, Cristiano cleared up the drama after the match, insisting that Wayne was a friend. Soon after the match, it was clarified that Rooney's red card was because of an infraction (stomping on Carvalho) and had nothing to do with Cristiano.

During Portugal's semifinal match against France, in which they lost by a score of 0-1, Cristiano was heavily booed by the crowd. They went on to also lose the third-place match against Germany, 1-3. To make matters worse, Cristiano was not given the competition's "Best Young Player" award (it ended up being given to German, Lukas Podolski) because of a great deal of negative campaigning against him initiated by England fans. So while he performed well statistically, Cristiano's first World Cup stint was considered a tumultuous one.

Even with the 2006 World Cup in the rear view mirror, Cristiano experienced hostility from the English crowds. Aside from enduring booing during his 2006-07 campaign with United, he also experienced pressure from the English press. It had gotten so bad that he publicly contemplated leaving United because of this issue.

However, the tension cooled eventually, especially as Cristiano and Rooney were seen playing together and showing companionship on the field. In spite of the heightened scrutiny, Cristiano continued his cold-blooded play, especially in the clutch moments of games. After being booed all match by Reading fans, Cristiano came through with the equalizing goal in a 1-1 draw. His ability to channel the animosity towards him into inspiration to play even better became one of his biggest strengths as an athlete and is something that he would continue to showcase throughout his career.

Manchester United Coach, Sir Alex Ferguson, urged Cristiano to stay prior to the year's campaign, and his trust was rewarded by a breakout year. Not only did Cristiano break the twenty goal mark for the first time in his young career, but he also earned his first league title. One of the catalysts for this spectacular year was Cristiano being personally coached by Rene Meulensteen. Meulensteen encouraged him to become a less predictable player when making his attacks. Additionally, Meulensteen taught him how to incorporate his teammates more effectively, including how to call for the ball and how to find opportunities for simpler, less aesthetically pleasing goals.

Cristiano received the "Barclays Player of the Month" award in November and December of 2006. He became only the third player in the history of the Premier League (the other 2 were Dennis Bergkamp and Robbie Fowler) to win this award in two consecutive months. Cristiano finished the year off in dominant fashion, scoring three consecutive braces. In late February, he scored a dramatic winner versus Fulham, putting United nine points ahead in the league table. Once again, he performed valiantly in the FA Cup, including timely goals against Middlesbrough, Roma, and Watford. Additionally, he helped United defeat Manchester City by scoring the only goal in a 1-0 victory, giving United its first Premier League title in four years.

While they lost in the FA Cup final and the Champions League semifinal, the Premier League title meant the season was considered a huge success. Rewarded for his best season yet, Cristiano compiled some of the sport's most prestigious awards in 2007. These awards included the PFA's Players' Player of the Year award, Young Player of the Year award, and Fans' Player of the Year award.

Additionally, he was given the FWA Footballer of the Year award. Cristiano became the only player in the history of the sport to win all of these awards in a single season. In mid-April of 2007, Cristiano signed an extension worth thirty-one million pounds over the span of five years. As a team, Manchester United had eight players named to the PFA Premier League Team of the Year for 2006-07.

Cristiano's 2007-08 season started off in dramatic fashion, as he was ejected for a headbutt against Richard Hughes. Cristiano was given a three match ban for that incident. Despite his three game suspension, Cristiano got off to a hot start during that season, having scored thirteen goals by Christmas. He scored his first goal of the year against his former club, Sporting, in the form of a header. He also posted braces against Wigan, Blackburn, Fulham, and Everton. The second goal against Everton came on a penalty shot in the 88th minute.

In mid-January, Cristiano posted his first career hat-trick in a game against Newcastle United. He then tied his previous season high of twenty-three goals in a match against Reading. At the end of January, Cristiano drew great attention for his beautiful free kick against Portsmouth - an instant classic that critics say is one of the best free kicks they have ever seen. The goal was his second of the game. He put up another brace in a 5-1 victory over Newcastle United in late February.

Cristiano played his first game as captain of United on March 19th against Bolton, scoring both goals in a 2-0 victory. With the second goal of the match (and 33rd for the season), Cristiano set a new club record for the most goals in a single season by a midfielder, topping George

Best's record, which stood for over four decades. During United's championship run, Cristiano scored the equalizer against Middlesbrough, a penalty in a 2-1 victory against Arsenal, and the opening two goals against West Ham United. Topping off his excellent post-season run, Cristiano scored the first goal in United's 2-0 victory against Wigan to win their second straight Premier League title. He finished with 31 total goals in the Premier League.

In the 2008 UEFA Champions League, Cristiano scored the decisive goal against Olympique Lyonnais in the knockout stage of the tournament. During the quarterfinal match, he played at striker and scored a header against AS Roma. Despite the fact that Cristiano missed a penalty kick during the first leg, United advanced to the Champions League final by beating Barcelona, thanks to a solid team effort and a timely goal by Paul Scholes.

United was set to face their league rival, Chelsea, in the final match. Cristiano wasted no time making his presence felt, as he scored the opening goal in the twenty-sixth minute of play. After a Chelsea equalizer by Frank Lampard in the forty-fifth minute, the match ended at 1-1, after extra time. In a dramatic finish decided by penalties, the biggest moment of the match came when Chelsea captain, John Terry, missed his penalty which would have won them the title - after slipping on the pitch surface. With renewed hope in the shootout, United went on to take the victory by a score of 6-5 in penalty shots. After the match, Cristiano was named the UEFA Fans' Man of the Match.

For the year, Cristiano came in second in the 2007 Ballon d'Or, behind Kaka, and third in the FIFA World Player of the Year award, behind Kaka and Lionel Messi. After scoring a career-high thirty-one league goals, Cristiano was given the Premier League Golden Boot award, as well as the Premier League Player of the Season award. Additionally, he was given the PFA Players' Player of the Year and FWA Footballer of the Year award once more. To top off his accolade-filled season, Cristiano made the PFA Team of the Year for the third straight time.

Cristiano scored forty-two goals in all competitive play, only four shy of Law's club record of forty-six. As the top scorer in the Champions League, Cristiano was named the best forward and player of the tournament. He became the first winger to ever win the European Golden Shoe. After such an impressive season, Cristiano was now considered as one of the faces of the sport, having developed a large worldwide fan-base. He also began to accumulate influential sponsors and was routinely featured on the world's biggest sports media outlets.

Cristiano's meteoric rise was also evident in international play. In a 2007 friendly against Brazil, he was named captain of the Portuguese national team, making him one of the youngest players to hold such a distinction in international football. During Portugal's UEFA Euro 2008 qualifying matches, Cristiano scored eight goals. However, he only scored one goal during tournament play and the team was eliminated in the quarterfinal round against Germany by a score of 3-2.

Cristiano was named "Man of the Match" in the group stage victory over the Czech Republic. After the disappointing team effort, Portugal decided to make a coaching change, replacing Luiz Felipe Scolari with Carlos Queiroz. Upon his hiring, Queiroz named Cristiano as the permanent captain of the Portugal national team. His permanent captaincy would seal his reputation as the face of Portuguese football for years to come.

Just before the start of the 2008-09 season, Cristiano underwent ankle surgery, which put him on the sidelines for the next three months. Meanwhile, rumors of a transfer to Real Madrid continued to swirl. While the Galacticos has always been in the mix for Cristiano's services ever since his 2006 World Cup fiasco made him public enemy in England, the rumors linking him to a transfer to Spain only became stronger this year. It got to a point where even FIFA president Sepp Blatter got involved, due to Manchester United filing a tampering complaint against Real Madrid.

Cristiano made his return after ankle surgery in a mid-September UEFA Champions League group stage match against Villarreal. Showing a bit of rust, it wasn't until a week later that Cristiano scored his first goal of the year in a game against Middlesbrough in the third round of the League Cup. In late October, Cristiano looked to have regained his health, showing dominance on the field once again. In a 2-0 victory over West Ham, Cristiano scored both goals. Only three days later, he put up another brace in a 4-3 win over Hull City. In mid-November, Cristiano helped United rout Stoke City in a 5-0 victory, putting up another brace - with the goals being the 100th and 101st of his career with United.

Cristiano finally earned the Ballon d'Or in early December, a well-deserved honor. He became the first player from United to win the award since George Best did so in 1968. As a testament to how dominant Cristiano was during the campaign, the final vote count showed that he earned 446 points - 165 ahead of the runner-up, FC Barcelona's Lionel Messi. Cristiano would say that receiving this prestigious award was "one of the most beautiful days of [his] life".

Cristiano rode this personal and team momentum into a very successful next few months. He helped United beat Gamba Osaka in the semifinal round of the Club World Cup and then assisted on the winning goal against LDU Quito in the final round. He was awarded the Silver Ball as the second best player of the tournament (the Golden Ball was won by teammate Wayne Rooney). In mid-January, he became the first Premier League player to be named the FIFA World Player of the Year. In the process, he also became the first Portuguese player to win this award since Luis Figo in 2001.

Cristiano continued to perform at an elite level into May. During an April match against Tottenham, he helped lead United back from an 0-2 half-time deficit to win 5-2. By the end of the game, he had a brace - including the all-important third goal that pushed his team over the top. On May 10th, Cristiano scored what would turn out as his final goal for United, during a "Manchester Derby" match against Manchester City.

In the Champions League, Cristiano helped United defeat Chelsea, Porto, and Arsenal to earn a final round match-up with Barcelona. He scored a forty yard game-winner to defeat Porto - still one of the greatest goals in his fine career. He was even given the first-ever FIFA Puskas Award for the top goal of the year.

Against Arsenal, Cristiano scored two goals to help his team reach the UEFA Champions League final for the second straight year.

However, United was shut out by Barcelona by a score of 0-2. Barcelona, a loaded squad led by Lionel Messi and coached by Pep Guardiola, would soon begin their reign as a dominant force in European football.

Cristiano appeared in fifty-three matches over all competitions, and finished the year with twenty-six goals. While this was down from the 42 he scored during the previous year, it was still a highly impressive performance. For his efforts, he was named to the PFA Team of the Year for the fourth consecutive time.

In June of 2009, Manchester United accepted an offer of eighty million pounds from Real Madrid in exchange for Cristiano's rights. Once the transfer was complete, Cristiano thanked his coach Ferguson, giving him credit for helping him become a better player and a better man. He even went so far as calling Ferguson his "father in sport".

Despite an abrupt ending to his time with Manchester United, there is no doubt that Cristiano is one of the best players to ever play for the organization. Together, they experienced a great deal of success during his years with the club. In total, United won three Premier League titles, one FA Cup title, two Football League Cup titles, one UEFA Champions League title, and one FIFA Club World Cup title, all during Cristiano's stint. Also, during his Manchester United phase, Cristiano grew from a ball of potential into one of the best players in the world. In the end, it will be remembered by fans as a short but highly successful partnership.

Real Madrid confirmed the signing of Cristiano Ronaldo on July 1st, 2009. The deal that Real Madrid and Manchester United agreed upon made him the most expensive footballer in history. The eighty million pound contract given to him was set to span over six years, with a buyout option pegged at 1 billion pounds.

After being publicly announced as a Real Madrid player, Cristiano was presented the number 9 by no less than Real Madrid legend Alfredo Di Stefano. Cristiano's arrival evoked a great deal of enthusiasm from Real Madrid's fan-base. In fact, more than 80,000 fans showed up at his opening press conference at his new home field, Santiago Bernabeau Stadium. This was considered as a world record, beating Diego Maradona's opening press conference for Napoli in 1984.

Cristiano quickly showed that Real Madrid's money was well-spent, as he became the first player ever to score in his first four La Liga appearances. In mid-September, Cristiano scored two free kicks in a 5-2 victory over Zurich, marking his first Champions League goals with his new team.

After injuring his ankle on October 10th, Cristiano stayed out of play until the end of November. His time away from the field caused him to miss both of Real Madrid's Champions League matches with Milan.

After a successful rehabilitation process, Cristiano returned in a 0-1 defeat to Barcelona. A week later, Cristiano was sent off the field for the first time with Madrid, though the team won 4-2 against UD Almeria. On May 5th, he scored his first hat-trick as a part of Real Madrid, in a match against Mallorca. The team finished the year without a trophy, but Cristiano and Gonzalo Higuain combined for fifty-three goals on the year - becoming the highest scoring duo in the club's history.

The emergence of Higuain alongside Cristiano showed that Real Madrid's chemistry was building quickly and had great promise for the future. In his first season with Real Madrid, Cristiano finished second in both the FIFA World Player of the Year and Ballon d'Or awards.

In June, Cristiano participated in the 2010 World Cup as part of team Portugal, once again playing the role of team captain. Showing a much-evolved game, he was named the "Man of the Match" in all three of Portugal's group matches (against Cote d'Ivoire, North Korea, and Brazil). During the knockout stages, they drew Spain as their opponent in the round of 16, Despite showing growth as a team, Portugal lost in the Round of 16 at a score line of 0-1. Spain, boasting a loaded and well-functioning squad at the peak of their powers, ended up winning the World Cup that year.

After Raul departed Real Madrid in the summer of 2010, Cristiano was given the number 7 jersey. Once again, he had to live up to the expectations of following a legendary jersey number. Raul, the long-time team captain of Real Madrid, who had a massive fan base, had worn that jersey for many years and accomplished a lot of things for the squad while doing so. After a less-than-spectacular first season for Real Madrid (in terms of team success) and an early exit at the World Cup,

Cristiano entered the 2010-11 season with great drive and motivation.

In late October, he scored a career-high four goals in a game against Racing de Santander. The monster game also highlighted a personal run of six consecutive matches with at least one goal scored. During that span, Cristiano put up eleven goals, marking the most he had ever scored in a single month. He followed up this great October with another excellent month, posting a hat-trick against Athletic Bilbao for his second La Liga hat-trick of the season.

Before the year's end, he went on to score another hat-trick against Levante in the Copa Del Rey. Along with Cristiano's personal dominance, Real Madrid was noticeably finding its stride as a team. It seemed like almost every other game was a blowout in the last three months of 2010.

The momentum continued for Cristiano and the team in 2011. He scored two goals in a 3-2 victory against Getafe and then hat-tricks against Villarreal and Malaga soon-after. Cristiano injured a muscle during the 7-0 destruction of Malaga, which forced him to spend the next ten days on the sidelines. In April, he made his return and immediately went on another scoring streak. The most notable of those performances was scoring two goals in a Champions League quarterfinal match against Tottenham.

In the following few games, Cristiano showed the world why he will go down as one of the greatest players in the history of this sport. In the second edition of El Clasico, he raised his goal tally for the season to forty-one, while also extending his scoring streak to four games. Then, he scored the winning goal in the 103rd minute of the Copa del Rey final match against the same Barcelona squad - showing that his clutch gene from his previous stint was still alive and well.

As if that wasn't hot enough, Cristiano went blistering against Sevilla, scoring four goals in a 6-2 rout. The four goals rose his season total to forty-six, surpassing his previous personal record of forty-two in a single season. Only three days later, he posted another hat-trick in a 4-0 victory against Getafe.

In a mid-May match against Villarreal, Cristiano tied the La Liga record for the most goals in a single season with thirty-eight, a record co-held by Telmo Zarra and Hugo Sanchez. As you would expect by now, Cristiano did not intend to stop there, with one more league match remaining. On May 21st, he scored two more goals, becoming the first man in the history of La Liga to score 40 goals in a season.

Because of his sustained excellence throughout the 2010-11 season, Cristiano received the European Golden Shoe Award, becoming the first man to win the award in two different leagues. Not only did he put up very high totals but Cristiano was able to put up such totals with extreme efficiency. He set the record for most goals per minute at 1 per 70.7 minutes played.

Along with the high praise and the recognition within Europe, Cristiano was now a globally recognized athlete who transcended the sport of football. He was featured on Sports Illustrated, who called him "one of the world's best footballers" after he shattered his previous single-season scoring record of forty-two goals, finishing with fifty-three across all 2010-11 competitions.

Cristiano started the 2011-12 La Liga season the same way he ended the previous: with guns blazing. In Real Madrid's first game, he scored a hat-trick as part of a 6-0 rout at Real Zaragoza. He scored another hat-trick in a 6-2 victory vs. Rayo Vallecano, marking Cristiano's tenth with Real Madrid and his ninth in La Liga. A big moment for the team came in mid-December, when Cristiano scored a hat-trick to defeat

Sevilla, moving Real Madrid to the top of the league standings.

In the notable yearly awards, Cristiano finished third in the UEFA Best Player in Europe Award and second in Ballon d'Or. The top three finishers for both awards were Messi, Xavi, and Cristiano. And while they lost against Barcelona in the Copa Del Rey quarterfinals, both Cristiano and Real Madrid stayed on a roll.

In February, Cristiano's hat-trick propelled Real Madrid over Levante, giving the team a ten point lead over Barcelona in the standings. Not long afterwards, Cristiano became the second quickest player to reach one-hundred goals in La Liga - having done so in just three short seasons. To achieve this feat, he only needed 92 games, which was the second-fastest mark in the history of La Liga.

Then, Cristiano scored three goals and assisted on the last one in a 4-1 victory over Atletico

Madrid. This show of dominance propelled him over the forty goal mark in La Liga for the second consecutive season. With this feat, he became the only man to score forty or more goals in two seasons in the history of ANY European league. When he scored against Mallorca in the last match day of the season, Cristiano became the first player in history to score against every team in a single La Liga campaign.

For the season, Cristiano was able to score forty-six league goals and sixty goals in all competitions combined - breaking his own record. More importantly to him, Real Madrid won the league title and was playing with marvelous teamwork.

At Euro 2012, Cristiano faced immense pressure from the media and some spectators, who taunted him throughout the tournament. Given his record-setting form professionally, Portuguese fans expected him to show the same form while playing for flag and country. Also, his critics were ready to see him fail. He scored seven goals during Portugal's qualifying campaign. The team was chosen as part of Group B together with the Netherlands, Germany, and Denmark. The group was considered extremely competitive and even referred to by some as the "group of death".

In the first group match, Portugal lost to Germany 0-1. Ronaldo was criticized for not performing well and for showing frustration. Regardless, in the all-important final group match, Cristiano showed why he is considered a clutch player, scoring two goals to push the team to a 2-1 victory over the Netherlands. This victory allowed Portugal to advance to the quarterfinal round. Once again, Cristiano came through at the end for Portugal in their quarterfinal match, scoring a header in the 79th minute against the Czech Republic to take a 1-0 victory. Upon scoring the goal, Cristiano celebrated in front of a camera, saying "para ti" in a dedication to his son.

The team's semifinal match against defending World Cup champion Spain ended in controversial fashion. In the penalty shootout that ensued, Cristiano was slated to take the fifth penalty shot. This gamble was made by Portugal coach Paulo Bento, thinking he would need Cristiano's services more should the shootout go the distance.

However, that opportunity never came, as Spain won the shootout 3-1. With that loss, Portugal was eliminated from tournament play. Still, they took home the bronze medal in a tournament and most experts did not consider them making the semifinal round. Individually, Cristiano was named part of the Euro 2012 "Team of the Tournament" and finished the tournament tied with five other players for top goal scorer with 3 goals.

His next season with Real Madrid began on a high note, as the team won the Supercopa de Espana by defeating Barcelona on aggregate. Along the way, Cristiano then equalled the Real

Madrid record of scoring in five consecutive El Clasico matches and became the first player in Real Madrid history to score in 4 straight matches against Barcelona in their home stadium. In late August, it was announced that Cristiano was tied for runner-up with Messi in the 2011-12 UEFA "Best Player in Europe" award, just behind Andres Iniesta.

In September, Cristiano scored his first two goals of the league season while also recording his 150th goal for Real Madrid. Despite only being with the team for a few years, he had already become the tenth highest scorer in Real Madrid history. Cristiano scored a La Liga hat-trick at the end of the month, in a 5-1 victory over Deportivo La Coruna. He recorded his first career Champions League hat-trick in a 4-1 victory against Ajax. Then, he became the only player to score in six consecutive El Clasicos, after a brace against Barcelona.

A notable moment came on January 6th, when Cristiano scored a brace against Real Sociedad -

his first match as the team's captain. The next day, he was named runner-up to Messi in the Ballon d'Or for the fourth time. After a beautiful hat-trick against Celta Vigo in a Copa del Rey game, Cristiano scored another against Getafe in a game that also featured his 300th club goal.

In his 500th club appearance, Cristiano became the first non-Spaniard to captain a Real Madrid team in a Clasico, during a Copa Del Rey match against Barcelona. He would later face his former team Manchester United in a UEFA Champions League quarterfinal, scoring a goal to secure a 1-1 draw at home.

In late February, Cristiano posted another hat-trick in a game against Sevilla - the twenty-first of his career. In his first return to Old Trafford since his signing with Real Madrid, Cristiano scored the winning goal in a 2-1 victory against his former team. In a very honest response after the game, Cristiano said that he felt a little "sad" upon knocking his former team out of the Champions League. Not only did he defeat the team that saw him grow up; he also did so in front of the fans who used to support him greatly.

In March, Cristiano put up a brace against Celta Vigo to put him among the top twenty-five goalscorers in the history of La Liga - in only 127 games played. Of all the players in the top twenty-five, Cristiano had the highest average goals per game - at 1.08. In mid-March, Cristiano scored the 350th goal of his career.

The next career benchmark came when he scored his 200th goal for Real Madrid in early May. At the time of this accomplishment, Cristiano was sixth on the club's all-time scoring list. He was also the fastest to reach this mark, needing only 197 matches to complete the mark.

Cristiano's fourth season with Real Madrid concluded with him as the Champions League top goalscorer, with 12 goals. His season total featured fifty-five goals scored, including nineteen with his right foot, sixteen with his left foot, and nine with his head. This diversity in his scoring abilities furthered the notion that Cristiano was one of the most all-around scorers that the sport had ever seen.

Real Madrid was eliminated in the semifinal round of the UEFA Champions League by eventual runner-up Borussia Dortmund. They were also unable to defend their La Liga title, coming in second place to Barcelona. To top it off, Real Madrid also lost in the Copa Del Rey final, 2-1 against Atletico Madrid, with Cristiano earning a red card.

In spite of the massive success and fanfare Cristiano enjoyed as a Real Madrid player, rumors still circulated about him being unhappy. All kinds of reasons were pointed out, from the fact that they won no titles the previous year to rumors of infighting in the locker room. After a great deal of speculation regarding Cristiano's future by the media, including a possible return to the English Premier League, the rumors were finally put to an end when he and the club agreed to a new contract in mid-September. The deal extended the relationship until 2018, featuring a salary of seventeen million pounds per year. This new deal made Cristiano the highest paid player in all of football.

Immediately after signing the extension, Cristiano posted the second hat-trick of his Champions League career in a 6-1 group stage victory against Galatasaray. This was followed by a brace against Getafe CF - the second goal coming from a beautiful back-heel kick. These performances moved Cristiano into fifth place on the Real Madrid all-time scoring list with 208 goals. In late October, he became the Champions League's third all-time leading goalscorer with fifty-seven career goals, when he scored twice during a 2-1 victory over Juventus.

Cristiano's ascent up the Champions League record book continued when he set the record for most goals in a calendar year (14). Then, he became second on La Liga's career hat-trick list, upon scoring his nineteenth hat-trick in La Liga play. As Cristiano was going through another one of his special runs (he had scored 32 goals in 22 matches in all campaigns at that point), he experienced a muscle strain in a game against Almeria in late November.

However, he returned in time for the team's Champions League group stage match against Copenhagen. He scored once in their 2-0 victory, achieving the record for most goals in the group stages with 9 total. After scoring a header in the final match of the calendar year, Cristiano finished with sixty-nine goals in fifty-nine appearances during 2013.

After arguably his best calendar year yet, Cristiano returned in the same blistering form after the winter break. He posted a brace during a 3-0 victory over Celta Vigo, marking his 400th professional career goal with club and country matches combined. In a show of class, Cristiano dedicated his brace to Eusebio, who passed away only two days prior to the match.

A big breakthrough moment came in mid-January when Cristiano finally beat Messi in the Ballon d'Or voting, having lost to the Argentine each of the previous four years. The honor was well-deserved and it cemented Cristiano's place as one of the all-time great players. This is not only because he won this prestigious award twice now, but also because he had been in the discussion for the award for most of his career. Furthermore, Cristiano became one of only ten players in the history of the sport to win the award multiple times.

After a brace against Schalke 04, Cristiano became the first player to score ten or more goals in three consecutive Champions League seasons. Another notable career accomplishment that shows Cristiano's sustained excellence was when he scored the only goal against Malaga in mid-March. It made Cristiano the first player to score twenty-five goals in five consecutive league seasons. On

March 29th, Cristiano equaled Messi's record of scoring in ten straight games.

After being forced to miss four matches due to a thigh injury, Cristiano returned to action in the Champions League semifinal first leg match against Bayern Munich. He then recorded his 100th goal at Santiago Bernabeau in a brace against Osasuna. Upon scoring two more goals against Bayern Munich in late April, Cristiano set a new record for most goals in a single Champions League season with 16.

Finally, he scored a back-heeled volley in the last few minutes to bring his goal total to fifty for the fourth straight season. This spectacular and timely goal earned Cristiano the LFP "Best Goal" award, a new accolade that is given to the best goal of the season.

Real Madrid finally reached their goal of taking the Champions League, by defeating cross-town rivals Atletico Madrid 4-1, at extra time. This victory was dubbed as the "La Decima", as it marked Real Madrid's 10th European Cup championship.

It was a match that was much closer than the score suggests, with Real Madrid's Sergio Ramos forcing extra time with an injury time goal. Real Madrid went on to dominate extra time by scoring 3 more goals.

At this point, Cristiano became the only man in history to score in and win two European Cup finals as part of two different teams. The tournament concluded with Cristiano as the top goal scorer for the second straight year, with a new record of seventeen goals during the season. He was awarded the Pichichi, as the top goalscorer in Spain, and won the European Golden Shoe along with Luis Suarez of Liverpool.

The 2014 FIFA World Cup and its preceding qualifying matches provided Cristiano additional opportunities to add to his already-gaudy international credentials. During the qualifying tournament, Ronaldo scored 8 goals, overtaking the legendary Eusebio in the list of Portugal's all-time leading scorers.

The second leg of their qualifying match against Sweden saw him score 4 goals, making him Portugal's all-time leading goal scorer. In spite of the records and the seemingly fine form, Cristiano was limping towards the World Cup, suffering from a thigh muscle injury plus patellar tendinitis on his left leg. With their campaign largely sitting on his shoulders, he still chose to play for his country. As their captain and face of their football program, he motivated himself not to go down without a fight.

In the group stages, Portugal was drawn together with Germany, USA, and Ghana. Often during the tournament, Cristiano left early to ice his knee while he received individualized training sessions. While not playing 100 percent, he played all 90 minutes in their first match against Germany. It ended with a loss, 4-0, and more questions swirled around his fitness for the tournament.

Still, he played on. Cristiano assisted on a late goal by Varela to help Portugal pull off a 2-2 draw against USA. He would then score the winning goal in their 2-1 victory against Ghana. In spite of his best efforts, Portugal did not made it to the knockout rounds due to goal difference. Germany ended up winning that tournament by beating Argentina in the finals.

Still not fully recovered from his injuries, Cristiano returned to Real Madrid and helped them win the UEFA Super Cup against Sevilla 2-0, with him scoring both goals. At the start of the 2014-15 La Liga season, he was awarded the UEFA Best Player in Europe award. From there, he went on a scoring spree, scoring one hat trick after another. At this point, he was attacking all kinds of scoring records. To encapsulate his incredible start, he made a La Liga record 15 goals in 8 matches.

On December 6th, 2014, Cristiano became the fastest-ever to reach 200 goals in La Liga play, after a victory against Celta Vigo, needing only 178 games to accomplish the feat. During that same game, he broke the La Liga record for most career hat tricks with his 23rd. Cristiano helped Real Madrid win the 2014 FIFA Club World Cup, the 4th championship they won within the calendar year. By the end of the year, he won the FIFA Ballon D'Or for the third time. He was the third person (after Ronaldo and Zinedine Zidane) to win this prestigious award 3 times.

In a UEFA Champions League quarterfinal match against Schalke 04, Cristiano grabbed the record for most goals in UEFA club competitions, with 78. At the same time, he also became the Champions League all-time leading scorer, sharing the record with Barcelona rival, Lionel Messi.

By April, he became the first man in football history to score 50 or more goals in 5 different seasons. On May 2nd, he broke Alfredo di Stefano's Real Madrid hat trick record with his 29th. He completed the year with a career-high 61 goals in all competitions, allowing him to win the Pichichi and the European Golden Shoe for the season. In spite of his efforts, Real Madrid came up empty, failing to win any championships for the season.

After the end of the La Liga campaign, Cristiano played for Portugal in UEFA Euro 2016 qualifying matches. He tied the all-time European competition record with his 22nd goal, when he scored a last-minute goal in Portugal's 1-0 victory against Denmark. He broke this record when he scored again in a 1-0 win against Armenia. With his 23rd goal (and counting) for Portugal in European competitions (including qualifiers), Cristiano now holds the solo record for most goals in this competition.

In spite of coaching turmoil in Real Madrid, Cristiano still showed his dominant self. On October 17th, 2015, he became Real Madrid's all-time leading goal scorer with his 324th goal in a 3-0 victory in La Liga against Levante. To celebrate this achievement, the team gave him a trophy. He also broke his own record by scoring 11 goals in the group stage of the Champions League. He finished the year as runner-up for the 2015 Ballon D'Or award.

Chapter 3:

Personal Adult Life

In addition to being one of the best athletes in the world, Cristiano is also one of the most interesting. His personal life, though he likes to keep it private, shows that he has diverse interests and loves to feel the connection with his fans. He has also set all kinds of trends both on and off the pitch, showing how large his influence is on the global scale.

In 2005, when Cristiano was only twenty years of age, his father passed away from an alcohol-related liver condition. Because his father was the reason he got into the sport, along with the fact that the two held a close relationship, Cristiano was hit hard by the loss. In fact, his father's death made him make a vow to not drink alcohol.

Nevertheless, he continued to work as hard as ever on the football field, making his father proud of the player and man he would become. Only two years after his father's sudden passing, Cristiano dealt with another personal hardship when his mother struggled with breast cancer during 2007. Once again, going through another devastating personal setback allowed Cristiano to grow stronger as a man.

Cristiano became a father on June 17th, 2010. While not much is known about his son Cristiano (also known by his nickname Cristianinho), he personally took care of him, putting him under his full custody. The identity of Cristianinho's mother was never revealed, though it is possible that she's American as the child was born in the United States. As for relationships, Cristiano has never been married, though he's had his share of relationships, the most recent (and most famous) one being the Russian model, Irina Shayk. Appearing together in a Spanish version of Vogue Magazine in 2014, they announced their split in January 2015.

In 2006, Cristiano started a fashion boutique with the name "CR7". The business originally opened in Madeira but in only two years, expanded to Lisbon. The store features beautiful clothing that will be sure to make anyone stand out in a crowd. They incorporate diamond-studs, leather pockets, and loafers. In addition to men's clothing, the store also sells outfits for women. Along with famous fashion designer, Richard Chai, Cristiano partnered with JBS Textile Group in 2013 to create a range of underwear.

In addition to his own clothing boutique, Cristiano has participated in endorsements for other major clothing brands. His chiseled body and good looks have always made him a no-brainer as a possible model-athlete. However, combine it with his world-class skills, and you get the ultimate product endorser. Most notable of these endorsements was when he was named a "spokesmodel" for Emporio Armani in late

2009. In this deal, he has modeled all kinds of Armani garments, ranging from jeans to underwear.

He is also currently signed with sportswear giant Nike. Arguably its most recognizable star in Europe (if not the world), he is one of the most current faces of Nike Football, together with other superstars such as Neymar, Wayne Rooney, and Zlatan Ibrahimovic. He has even appeared in other Nike promotional efforts with top endorsers from other sports, such as LeBron James, Rafael Nadal, and Manny Pacquiao.

Cristiano has worn the Nike Mercurial boots for his entire career and has been highly influential in Nike's staying power in the football scene. Currently, he has his own shoe line with Nike, the latest being the "Mercurial Superfly CR7".

As one of the most marketable athletes in the world for close to a decade, Cristiano has also signed endorsement deals with companies such as Coca-Cola, Motorola, KFC, Fly Emirates, and Tag Heuer, among others. In 2012, SportsPro ranked Cristiano as the fifth most marketable athlete in the world. In 2014, Repucom listed him as the most marketable footballer in the world.

Cristiano's popularity amongst casual sports fans can be demonstrated by his presence on social media. In 2010, he became the first sportsperson to ever reach fifty million followers on Facebook. In 2014, he became the first sportsperson to reach one hundred million followers on Facebook. In fact, he is just second overall (the first one was celebrity Shakira) to reach the 100-million mark in number of followers. Likewise, he is also the most followed athlete on Twitter and Instagram as of 2015. In December 2013, he even launched a dedicated social networking site and mobile app, Viva Ronaldo.

Over the years, Cristiano has been bestowed all kinds of unique accolades. As a show of respect, there are wax replicas of Cristiano at Madame Tussauds London and the Madrid Wax Museum. He has also been given praise by the President of Portugal, Anibal Cavaco Silva, who distinguished Cristiano to the rank of Grand Officer of the Order of Prince Henry. This rank shows Cristiano's contributions to Portugal, especially as an ambassador in the world of professional sports.

In 2013, Cristiano was selected by Sporting, the Portuguese squad where he started his professional career, to be the 100,000th member of the club. A bronze statue of him, created by world-renowned artist Ricardo Madeira Velasco, was unveiled in Funchal on December 21st, 2014. A group of astronomers led by Portuguese David Sobral named a galaxy "CR7" (Cosmos Redshift 7), done in tribute to Cristiano.

Because of his scintillating performance in football, Cristiano is considered as one of the most recognized athletes in the world. Multiple lists made by reputable sports research companies listed him at or near the top of lists of the world's most marketable athletes. In April of 2014, Cristiano was named as part of the prestigious "Time 100" list. This is Time Magazine's annual list of the one hundred most influential people in the world.

Because of his exciting playing style and global popularity, Cristiano has become a fan favorite in football video games as well. He was on the cover for Konami's Pro Evolution Soccer series, specifically the 2008, 2012, and 2013 versions. In his latter two appearances, he was also involved in the promotional side of the game's release. At the same time, he also appeared on the cover of EA Sports' soccer video games, namely the FIFA series and FIFA Street. In late 2011, Cristiano worked with RockLive to launch an iPhone game entitled "Heads Up with Cristiano", a big hit with his fans.

Due to his ventures and accomplishments both on and off the pitch, Cristiano is considered to be one of the world's richest athletes. Aside from the record salary he enjoys at Real Madrid, he also makes a ton of cash from his endorsements and business ventures. In fact, Forbes listed him as the world's highest-paid football player, with his overall payout from the 2014-15 season totaling at $79 million. He is the second highest earning athlete in the world, finishing just behind boxing superstar, Floyd Mayweather Jr.

Chapter 4:

Philanthropic/Charitable Acts

Cristiano has used his fame and global platform for more than just personal glory, he has also made it a point to give back to those who are less fortunate. Being charitable has always been something innate to him, doing these acts even when he wasn't considered as a superstar. Even now that he has become very famous, this trait has not changed one bit.

It can be noticed that Cristiano does not have any tattoos unlike some of his contemporaries such as Lionel Messi and Neymar. Some may think that it is a matter of fashion, but actually it is not. Ronaldo is actually an active blood donor, donating his own blood for charity several times a year. He understands that by getting inked, that would make him ineligible for making such donations. His love for giving his own blood is ultimately the reason why he has shied away from getting any tattoos.

Cristiano is known for being a very charitable man, even during the early part of his career. This was first put into display soon after the 2004 Indian Ocean earthquake and tsunami. Inspired by seeing Martunis, an eight year old boy wearing a Portugal jersey while being stranded for nineteen days after his entire family was killed, Cristiano decided to visit Aceh, Indonesia in order to raise funds to help rebuild the community.

Cristiano also showed great compassion for his hometown of Madeira, Portugal. Fresh from winning a libel suit against a British tabloid, Cristiano donated the funds to a charity based in Madeira. Cristiano also donated 100,000 pounds to a local hospital that helped in saving his mother's life in her fight against breast cancer. His main aim with the donation is for the hospital to build a cancer center for the island. A year later, he made a show of support for the 2010 Madeira flood victims, playing in a charity match, which featured FC Porto and players from Portuguese teams, Maritimo and Nacional.

He sold his 2011 Golden Boot for 1.5 million pounds, with the full proceeds coming from the sale used to fund schools for children in Gaza. He was also a part of FIFA's "11 for Health" program. The program's purpose is to help raise awareness regarding drug addiction, HIV, and obesity, among the youth. He also became the new Global Artist Ambassador for "Save the Children", in hopes to help challenge obesity and child hunger issues. He is also an ambassador for "The Mangrove Care Forum", an organization in Indonesia created to raise awareness in mangrove conservation. He also participated in FIFA's "11 against Ebola" program in 2014.

Cristiano takes a very active role in giving back, as showcased by his commitment to certain individuals. Upon learning that a ten month old boy needed brain surgery, Cristiano auctioned his signed jersey and boots, then decided to write a personal check for $83,000 to cover the operation costs, then offered to pay $8,000 a visit for follow up treatment. He has also paid for a nine year old terminally ill cancer patient to undergo a pioneering treatment for the treatment of his condition.

While he's been highly active in community and goodwill projects, not many people know about the many acts of kindness and charity Cristiano Ronaldo has done over the years. It is important for us to understand Cristiano's philosophy when it comes to philanthropy so that we can become more like him.

First off, it is important to understand that because Cristiano grew up in humble beginnings, he understands the importance of money and how it can drastically change one's life. He also knows that if it were not for the help of some influential people during his formative years, namely his father, mother, and coaches, he would not have become a great footballer, or even a professional. Most importantly, he has been on both sides of the coin, no pun intended, when it comes to finances - and he hasn't forgotten about that.

While the media loves to publicize the happenings of Cristiano's life, as it makes for promising click-bait, Cristiano is actually not proactively public in his philanthropic efforts. He prefers to give back and support causes that he believes in, letting the media coverage fall where it may. Another key pillar in his philosophy is that he believes giving away feels just as good as receiving. He has stated that every time he gives, he inevitably receives more.

By adopting these mindsets and lessons, we too can become more philanthropic and make a difference in our own circles of influence!

Chapter 5:

Legacy, Potential & Inspiration

As a player profile, Cristiano is widely regarded as one of the best two-way players in the entire world. Alongside Lionel Messi, the two are considered by most to be the best players of this generation and all-time greats. Cristiano's attacking style, whether as a striker or winger, has drawn fan attention since the time he became a professional.

He possesses the full offensive repertoire, using pace, dribbling, positioning, and is a top free kicker. Because of his wide skill set and deep understanding of the game, he is able to play on either wing as well as in the center of the pitch. Needless to say, Cristiano poses a problem for opposing players.

In addition to his obvious physical gifts, Cristiano is known to be a mentally sharp and creative player. He incorporates great vision and natural instincts, as well as an innate ability to predict plays. While he is a right footed player, Cristiano has become confident using either foot in shooting, dribbling, or passing - through years of practice.

What makes Cristiano a transcendent superstar in addition to his strong knowledge and application of the fundamentals, is the way that he incorporates flair into his style of play. He has been known to use flashy moves in one on one situations, sometimes even splitting double and triple teams with them. He is supremely accurate in set piece situations and is also known for his ability to bend free kicks.

Standing at over six feet tall and possessing notable strength and jumping ability for a footballer, he is also able to win battles in the air.

Whether he is scoring a goal via header or just establishing position, there is no doubt that Cristiano's physical abilities give him advantages on the field. While he has always possessed a lanky build, he has noticeably put on some muscle mass during his time as a professional. These physical gifts, combined with his impeccable skill and competitive spirit, has made Cristiano a matchup nightmare, with or without the ball.

Many of his teammates, coaches, and legends of the game alike, have given high praise regarding Cristiano's work ethic. It would be naive for anyone to believe that Cristiano has stayed among the top five players in the world for the greater part of the last decade without an incredible hunger and love for improving his skills. His drive comes from wanting to be one of the best players to ever play the game, while also being a great role model during his time on earth - a surefire recipe to becoming a name that will stand the test of time.

Just like most polarizing top athletes in the world, Cristiano must deal with media sources that are seemingly always trying to create drama or controversial headlines. However, while these media sources may receive some short term attention for their name-calling and stone-throwing, Cristiano is slowly building a legacy that can not be torn down. The numbers, the accolades, and the combined individual and team success just shows that he's a true winner.

This deadly combination of physical traits, football skill, and mental toughness allows him to visualize and execute plays that others think are impossible. In fact, his greatness is on such a level that spectators, teammates, and even opponents expect something to happen every time he touches the ball. It doesn't matter if it's just the first minute of the match or in a crucial play with the game on the line. When Cristiano Ronaldo is playing football, you can expect nothing less than greatness.

When talking about greatness, one of the most effective ways to measure it is based on statistics. As some would say, football, just like most sports, is a game of numbers. When it comes to scoring, he has only few equals. Cristiano is currently the all-time leading scorer in Real Madrid history. He's also the fastest in Real Madrid history to score 200 goals, doing it within 197 games with the club.

He is also the fastest player in La Liga history to score 200 goals, doing it in 178 games. In the Champions League, he is the record holder for most goals in a single season with 17, during their championship-winning run in 2014. If you are the type of person that holds a players numbers in high regard, then there is no question about the greatness of Cristiano Ronaldo's career.

As they say, action speaks louder than words. As a man who has just turned thirty, Cristiano is inspiring an entire generation through his focus on giving back and living as an example that hard work and dedication are the keys to building a successful life - no matter the profession.

He is now considered by many fans and analysts as one of the greatest Real Madrid players of all time. Considering the number of greats who have played for this team (Alfredo di Stefano, Raul, Zinedine Zidane, Iker Casillas, etc.), that is no small feat. With still years to add on to his legacy (it will take something extreme to dislodge him from that team), one can only imagine Cristiano making more memories and records at the Santiago Bernabeau.

In his native Portugal, Cristiano is considered a national treasure. While he is still active in the international game, the current team captain of the Portuguese national team (he has held that title since 2008) is considered as Portugal's greatest footballer of all time.

This was given no less than by the Portuguese Football Federation during its 100th anniversary celebration. While the chase is still on for that World Cup title that will cement his place among the absolute greatest, his resume while playing for Portugal is simply undeniable. His path to the title is considerably tougher as Portugal is not really considered as a football powerhouse, but this has not stopped him from performing his best. As long as he is there performing and inspiring his squad, Portugal will always remain a threat to compete for international championships.

Cristiano Ronaldo has already accomplished all kinds of things in his playing career. Breaking records left and right while also displaying his dominant presence for more than a decade since he first turned pro, his credentials both on and off the pitch are simply incredible.

What makes things even more amazing is that while his resume makes him one of the most decorated football players ever, he still has more than enough left in the tank to pile on his records and even create new ones. By the time his career is up, his name will definitely be up there among the best of the best. While his legacy is very much secured, it is also still being written at the same time.

The legacy is already there. The potential is still there. And he is still there to be an inspiration for all. He is Cristiano Ronaldo. Truly, one of the world's best.

Conclusion

Hopefully this book was able to help you gain inspiration from the life of Cristiano Ronaldo, one of the best football players in the world.

Cristiano serves as a great representative for Portugal, Europe, and the sport of football. His respectful demeanor and understanding of the legends before him makes it very hard for someone to dislike him. Additionally, he is able to keep fans glued to the television because they know that any time he plays, there is a possibility that he will make history.

Cristiano has inspired so many people because he is the star who never fails to connect with fans and give back to the less fortunate. Noted for his ability to dominate the competition on any day, he is a joy to watch on the field. Last but not least, he's remarkable for remaining simple and firm with his principles in spite of his immense popularity.

Hopefully you've learned some great things about Cristiano in this book and are able to apply some of the lessons that you've learned to your own life! Good luck in your journey!

74840790R00051

Made in the USA
Lexington, KY
16 December 2017